William

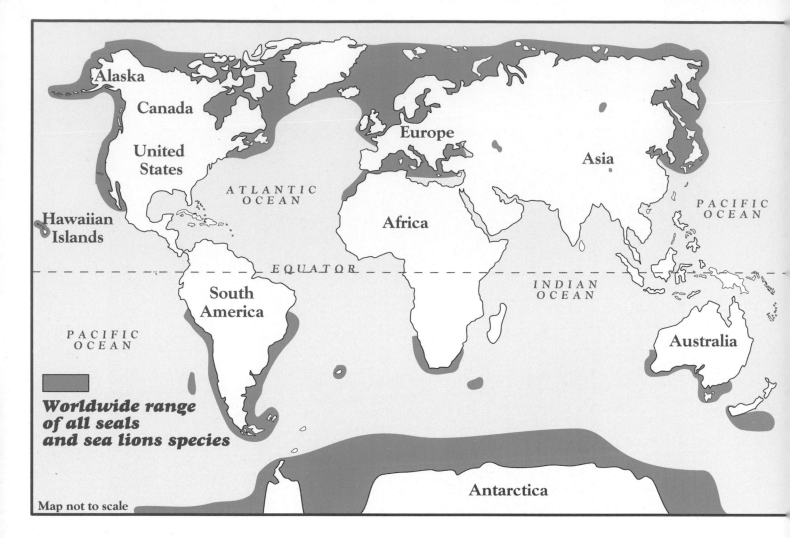

Alaska

Canada

United
States

ATLANTIC
OCEAN

Europe

Asia

PACIFIC
OCEAN

Hawaiian
Islands

Africa

EQUATOR

INDIAN
OCEAN

South
America

PACIFIC
OCEAN

Australia

**Worldwide range
of all seals
and sea lions species**

Antarctica

Map not to scale

*n*oisy, fishy, yet somehow lovable, seals are marine mammals which live in the waters around every continent on the globe. Numbering over 30 species, they range from the sleek grace of the Australian sea lion, pictured opposite, to the droll and bulky walrus. Most prefer colder seas for the good fishing they find. Those that favor Arctic waters? Fur seals, Steller sea lions, plus harp, ringed, and gray seals. In the Antarctic live Ross, leopard, Weddell, and crabeater seals. Most common pinniped in the world, the misnamed crabeater moves faster on land than any other seal – but not in pursuit of crab. Its favorite food is krill.

A few seals even like warmer waters. The rare monk seal frolics off the Hawaiian Islands and in the Mediterranean. Every continent boasts different seal species, from fur seals in South Africa to giant elephant seals on the South American coast.

The pinniped with the widest range may be the harbor or common seal. Often seen around the British Isles and other Northern European countries, it also makes its home around Japan and along the east and west coasts of North America from Mexico to Canada.

In this book, you'll meet three species that typify the pinniped way of life: harbor seals, California sea lions, and elephant seals.

SEALS & SEA LIONS

An Affectionate Portrait

CLOSE-UP
A Focus on Nature

SILVER BURDETT PRESS

© 1995 Silver Burdett Press
Published by Silver Burdett Press.
A Simon & Schuster Company
299 Jefferson Road, Parsippany, NJ 07054
Printed in the United States of America
10 9 8 7 6 5 4 3 2 1

Library of Congress
Cataloging-in-Publication Data
León, Vicki.
Seals and sea lions:an affectionate portrait/by Vicki
León;photographs by Frank Balthis.
p. cm. -- (Close up)
ISBN 0-382-24889-9 (LSB)
ISBN 0-382-24890-2 (SC)
1. Harbor seal--Pacific Coast (North America)--
Juvenile literature. 2. California sea lion--Pacific Coast
(North America)--Juvenile literature. 3. Northern elephant
seal--Pacific Coast (North America)--Juvenile literature.
[1. Harbor seal. 2. California sea lion. 3. Northern ele-
phant seal. 4. Seals (Animals). 5. Sea lions.] I. Balthis,
Frank, ill. II. Title. III. Series: Close up (Parsippany, N.J.)
QL737.P6L54   1994
599.74'6--dc20   94-31827
                                                        CIP
                                                          AC

TEXT
Vicki León

PHOTOGRAPHS
Frank Balthis

ADDITIONAL PHOTOGRAPHS
Ralph A. Clevenger, Howard Hall,
Richard Hansen & W.E. Townsend, Jr.

BOOK DESIGN
Ashala Nicols-Lawler

ILLUSTRATIONS & MAPS
Cathi Von Schimmelmann

SILVER BURDETT PRESS

© 1995 Silver Burdett Press
Published by Silver Burdett Press.
A Simon & Schuster Company
299 Jefferson Road, Parsippany, NJ 07054
Printed in the United States of America
10 9 8 7 6 5 4 3 2 1

WHAT ARE PINNIPEDS?

"Pinniped" – meaning "feather- or fin-footed " – describes a family of chubby marine mammals often lumped together as seals. The family includes walruses, eared seals such as the sea lion, and earless or "true" seals. In this book, we'll be looking at the pinnipeds most often seen along the Pacific coast of North America: harbor seals, California sea lions, and northern elephant seals.

About 25 million years ago, the first eared seal made its appearance, having evolved from a bearlike ancestor. (True seals came somewhat later by way of an otterlike ancestor.) Today over 30 species of pinnipeds live in nearly every ocean of the world. These pinniped cousins have distinct looks and lives. They can be as massive as an 6,000-pound southern elephant seal, or as small as a 125-pound ringed seal. Some are quiet; others, non-stop vocalizers.

What do these family members have in common? First, they are comfortable in two worlds: on land and in the sea. They share a

3

Because pinnipeds spend so much time underwater, their nostrils are locked shut, not open. To inhale, a seal "snorts" its nostrils open. Front and back flippers vary among pinnipeds. Harbor seals have short, stubby foreflippers (pictured right), used to steer underwater and to pull the animal forward on land.

common body shape – muscular, sleek, well-padded with blubber. With these flippered bodies, pinnipeds flash through the water with acrobatic grace and speed. On land, we often find their movements amusing, but they don't do badly here, either. Some seals can slide 100 feet a minute on their bellies. There are two-ton pinnipeds that can climb steep sand dunes – even cliffs. Depending on species, pinnipeds haul out on land to rest, to mate, to give birth, to nurse pups, and to molt.

Pinnipeds are the world's finest deep-sea divers, descending as much as half a mile to catch their prey. (That's far deeper than almost any mammal or fish can dive.) Although they breathe air as we do, seals are ingeniously built to remain underwater for remarkable periods – 20 minutes is common, 43 minutes the longest we know about.

Pinnipeds share another, sadder bond. Like the great whales, many species were hunted by man to virtual extinction. With legal protection, most have now recovered. A few species are gone forever.

Since we have stopped killing pinnipeds for fur and dog food, we have found these trusting creatures to be valuable in other ways. Their intelligence and good nature make them the most frequently displayed marine mammal in captivity. Beyond entertainment, however, pinnipeds are proving their worth in cooperative ventures with humans. Seals and sea lions have learned to help divers in trouble, retrieve equipment and perform other tasks in water far beyond man's reach. Research into pinniped diving abilities has led to advances in medical science also.

Despite laws that now protect most pinnipeds, dangers remain. Every year, 100,000 of these animals die from eating plastic packaging tossed overboard by humans, or from entanglement in gillnets and other fishing gear. Chemical pollution and offshore oil exploration present other threats to the well-being of pinnipeds. Although we no longer kill pinnipeds deliberately, we have yet to stop killing the ocean itself.

Pinnipeds are opportunistic carnivores. They eat whatever is most plentiful in the area. Some are foods we eat and compete for, such as salmon and squid (pictured below).

It may look uncomfortable to us, but harbor seals find this balancing act easy and normal. They often haul out to rest on rocky outcroppings. Good visibility and quick access to deep water are what the harbor seals look for in a hauling-out spot. As they bask, they rub their flexible back flippers together.

rue seals – such as the harbor seal – have a mysterious appeal for humans. Perhaps it is their eyes: huge, alert, unwinking. Their eloquent gaze seems a bit out of place in such round, helpless-looking bodies.

Unlike the true seals further north, harbor seals were never slaughtered for fur or oil. Instead, in the middle of this century, many thousands of them were legally shot for bounty.

There are currently more than 300,000 harbor seals along the Pacific coast, from Alaska to Baja California. Despite their numbers, they are hard to spot. This shy, 250-pound pinniped tends to haul out onto terrain that resembles its markings. With its silvery-gray or brown coat, irregular black and white spots and relative immobility, the harbor seal is easily mistaken for a plump rock by the casual observer.

Harbor seals have very round heads and no external ears. On land, the harbor seal often rests on its belly, small foreflippers close to its body and back flippers in the air. To me, it looks like a fat little ship left high and dry by the tide. While basking, seals characteristically rub their back flippers together.

Harbor seals spend much time on land, hauling out on river banks, beaches, offshore reefs, rocky points and on manmade artifacts such as buoys and docks. They scoot along, inchworm fashion, and can cover a surprising amount of ground. Land is where harbor seals sleep. (They also rest underwater in the shallows, sometimes in large groups.) Harbor seals need to be on or near dry land to molt, give birth, nurse and care for their pups.

Like other pinnipeds, *Phoca vitulina* becomes a ballerina underwater. Spiraling like a corkscrew, the harbor seal swims with utmost ease, using its back flippers in a side-to-side motion to propel its body. The foreflippers serve to steer and grasp food.

A champion diver, the harbor seal sinks slowly to 600 feet and can hold its breath for 20 to 30 minutes. This is possible because of

Harbor seals live in Alaska, the Aleutian Island chain and as far north as the icy Bering Sea. They are found south as far as Mexico. Good seal-watching spots are found among the islands of southern Alaska; the Inland Passage of British Columbia; around Vancouver Island; Puget Sound and the San Juan Islands; the Columbia River; the Russian River mouth near Jenner; Point Reyes National Seashore; Seal Rock and San Francisco Bay; Bean Hollow State Beach and Pescadero State Beach in San Mateo County; Monterey; Pacific Grove; Point Lobos; and Montaña de Oro State Park near Morro Bay.

adaptations common to most pinnipeds. First is body build: ribs more parallel to spine so lungs can compress, a layer of blubber for heat retention, smooth skin and tear-drop shape for minimum water resistance. Internal organs are special too. The animal can slow its heartbeat and reduce blood flow so that oxygen use drops by one-third. Pinnipeds also have a high tolerance for carbon dioxide – one reason why humans have a difficult time in deep water.

Because nearly everyone has heard the non-stop noises of seals in captivity, we take it for granted they are as vocal in the wild. Not so. Harbor seals do occasionally bark, snort or moan, and young pups have a high "mom locator" cry.

Many pinnipeds migrate each year, but harbor seals do not. Their home base is their favorite hauling-out area. Like other pinnipeds, they breed and give birth at about the same time and place each year. Their pupping season falls between April and September, depending on locale.

Females give birth on land or water to a single pup, two to three feet long. This gangly baby has weak hindquarters but can nurse, swim and dive almost immediately. Harbor seals are devoted if short-term mothers through the four- to six-week nursing period. Sometimes, though, seal mothers "stash" pups on the beach while they swim or feed. Although these pups seem deserted, they are not. It is important not to feed or approach pups; your human scent may drive the mother away, leaving the pup to die.

By weaning, the pup has doubled its weight to around 50 pounds, grown a set of teeth and a layer of blubber and can look after itself quite well. Females now leave their pups and join the males. The social behavior of harbor seals is relaxed by pinniped standards. Males do not form harems or fight over females or territory. Instead, males and females form courtship pairs, leaping in and out of the water for some time. During this foreplay, the female bites the male on the neck and shoulders. (These "love bites" often leave visible scars.) The pair ultimately mates in the water. The female may mate with additional males; in any event, she usually becomes pregnant.

Most female pinnipeds have an ingenious mechanism called delayed implantation. It causes the fertilized egg to become dormant for several months. This allows the female to synchronize the birth of her next pup with the next pupping season, 12 months away. A female harbor seal can produce 15 or more pups in her lifetime.

By the time it is mature, a harbor seal needs to eat 5-10% of its body weight daily. Like all pinnipeds, they swallow most of their catch whole. Harbor seals eat many species of fish, octopus, squid, shrimp, crab and mollusks.

Whether wild or captive, a harbor seal lives 20 to 30 years. Their only enemies are killer whales, sharks and man. Pinnipeds are troubled by parasites which sometimes kill pups. Harbor seals, however, don't seem as afflicted as their cousins, the sea lions, which lose some of their number to parasites each year.

Harbor seals sometimes choose to sit where the tide is changing and let the water wash over them. Unlike the more placid elephant seals, harbor seals are nervous when humans approach too close.

Sea lions are called
Otariidae – "little
ears" – for good reason.
Their long leathery back
flippers are used as
rudders in the sea. On
land, the flippers turn
forward to walk upon.
Octopus (pictured right)
is an important food for
both sea lions and
harbor seals.

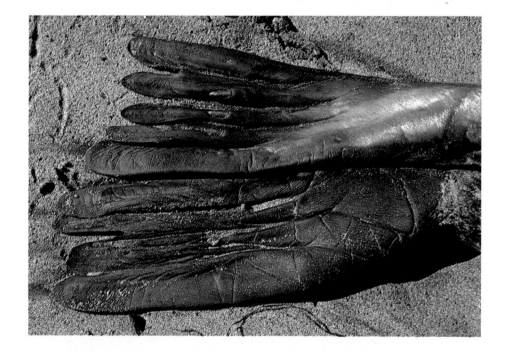

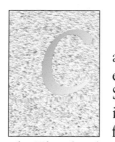

California sea lions belong to the *Otariidae* ("little ear") family. Other family members include the Steller sea lion and the fur seals. All of them have inch-long ears that look like curled leaves. Their faces are longer and more pointed than true or earless seals. The third trait that identifies the *Otariidae* is the way in which they move.

Underwater, sea lions and fur seals use their strong foreflippers to soar along, almost as a bird uses its wings. The back flippers extend behind and serve as rudders. Sea lions can achieve speeds of 15-25 mph underwater and dive to 450 feet or more.

On land, a sea lion turns its back flippers around and sits on them, much as a dog sits on its haunches. To move, it rears up on its foreflippers and galumphs along in a lunging, plunging gallop. Sea lions are so agile that they can scramble up cliffs and travel inland for some distance.

California sea lions are the noisy extroverts of the pinniped family – curious, clever, excitable. There are more of this species in captivity than any other pinniped. With its collie-dog muzzle, sleek brown body and sharp bark, it is the animal most people think of when the word "seal" comes to mind.

California sea lions like each others' company. They are often seen in tightly massed sunning groups. Juvenile or yearling sea lions, distinguished by their palomino coats, squirm among the darker adults. The biggest males monopolize the highest areas, posing for hours with magnificent, chest-bursting-with-pride displays.

Sea lions nurse their young up to six months – much longer than true seals. With their blondish fur, yearlings are easy to spot. They often snuggle up to adults of other species, especially the elephant seal (top pictures).

The adult males are readily identifiable by a bony growth on the head called the sagittal crest. As the animal matures, the crest becomes bigger and the hair on it, lighter. Females and juveniles have slimmer, doglike heads.

The most active and playful of the Pacific coast pinnipeds, California sea lions spend hours leaping in and out of the water. Sometimes you'll see groups of them floating asleep in the sea, their flippers extended into the air like shiny brown windmill blades. This is one way of regulating body temperature. Capillary-rich pinniped flippers can act as "solar panels" to warm or as "heat dumps" to cool the animals.

California sea lions can shoot out of the water and "fly" through the air, dolphin-style – sometimes in unison. This species also seems to enjoy body surfing, bubble chasing, kelp tossing and sparring in mock battles, using their long rubbery necks. Small wonder they readily learn ball-balancing, ladder-climbing, flipper-clapping and the other standard tricks in the performing pinniped repertoire.

In summer and fall, adult males migrate from the breeding grounds in search of food, accompanied by juveniles of both sexes. These migrations take them as far north as Canada and as far south as Mexico. They use Año Nuevo, the Monterey area and the Farallon Islands as rest stops. In contrast, females are stay-at-homes. Once they reach sexual maturity around age five, they remain in the rookeries or breeding/pupping areas year-round. The principal ones are the Channel Islands and the offshore islands of Baja California.

The dark pups are born in May and June. About ten days after birth, the females mate with the males. A territorial pinniped, the California sea lion when at his breeding prime establishes a territory on the beach in which he tries to corner ten or more females for

Steller sea lions (pictured this page) are heavier, furrier and quieter than California sea lions. When they do vocalize, it's a deep roar. They lack the head crest of their California cousins. Stellers prefer a more northern range, but the two species often sun together. Año Nuevo (pictured right) is a favorite spot. California sea lions don't look very lionish. The name may be derived from the Southern sea lion male, who has a striking tawny mane when dry.

mating purposes. First, though, he has to battle other males to gain a territory. Males who do not make it through the semi-finals are forced out and may never get to breed. What with battles and breeding, successful males do not eat for two months or so.

Once pups are born, females feed at sea and may be gone several days at a time between nursings. Meanwhile, the furry pups occupy themselves by learning to swim in tidepools, later soloing in the sea.

California sea lions are among the hungriest of pinnipeds, a fact which makes them readily trainable but a major nuisance to commercial fishing interests. Females weigh 200 to 400 pounds; males, 600 to 800 pounds. Both sexes can put away 15 to 20 pounds of food daily.

Their preferences include hake, squid, herring, octopus, crab and lamprey eel. The strangest item in their diet? Stones. Most pinnipeds have an odd habit of swallowing stones. But sea lions are the prize rock collectors. Sea lion stomachs have been found to contain up to 100 rocks, gravel to golf-ball size. Do the stones serve as ballast? As grist to help digest food or get rid of stomach parasites? No one knows. Some biologists believe the stones may ease hunger pangs during the long fasts that many pinnipeds go through in their breeding and nursing cycles.

There are many excellent spots to watch California sea lions (and occasionally, Steller sea lions) along the Pacific coast. They include: Sea Lion Caves in Oregon; Seal Rock near Cliff House in San Francisco; Fisherman's Wharf and the Coast Guard pier in Monterey; Point Lobos; Año Nuevo State Reserve; below the Big Sur cliffs; Santa Cruz Municipal Wharf; and Santa Cruz Lighthouse Point.

*a*n animal of extraordinary fascination, the elephant seal consists of two geographically distinct species. The southern elephant seal, largest of all pinnipeds, lives in icy Antarctic waters and on the lonelier islands and beaches of Argentina, New Zealand and the Antarctic continent. At near-extinction levels in the 19th century, the *Mirounga leonina* population may now exceed half a million animals. *Mirounga angustirostris*, the northern elephant seal, lives in the waters off Alaska and south to Baja California. Also reduced by unbridled slaughter to almost zero population around 1900, the northern elephant seal has slowly repopulated its range. An estimated 100,000 animals now group to breed on such island rookeries as Año Nuevo, the Farallones, the Channel Islands and the Mexican islands of Guadalupe and San Benito. Beginning at Año Nuevo in 1975, elephant seals have also established breeding areas on the mainland.

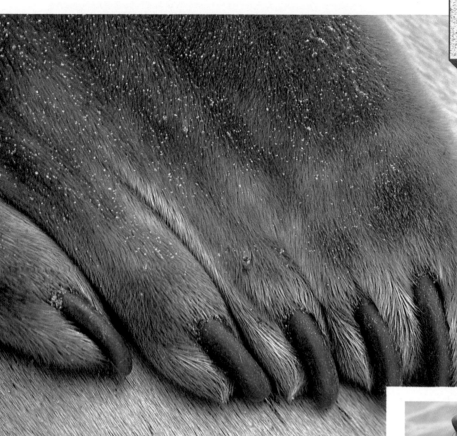

Why is the elephant seal so fascinating? For one thing, because its physical oddities are on such a grand scale. An adult male of the southern species may tip the scales at 6,000 pounds – the size of a truck. Northern animals are somewhat trimmer: between 1,000 and 1,500 pounds for a female, 3,000 to 5,000 pounds for a male. Nearly a ton of that weight consists of blubber. In sealing days, hunters obtained about 150 gallons of oil from the boiled-down blubber of each adult male.

Then there's that nose. As pups, all elephant seals have round faces, huge adorable eyes, and pointed muzzles with a couple of nostrils at the end. As the males grow older, their noses go from pug to Pinocchiolike. By the time an elephant seal reaches sexual maturity at age five or so, that nose has become a lumpy, dangling proboscis, one to two feet long. Unlike the trunk of a land elephant, this snout cannot manipulate food or do much of anything except act as a male hood ornament. Homely as it may appear to us, the nose on the male proclaims his masculinity. The bigger it is, the higher he ranks – and the more likely it is that he will father new little pug-nosed pups.

All pinnipeds vocalize but elephant seals produce a symphony of the most varied sounds imaginable. "Symphony" is definitely the wrong word. Among other things, elephant seals snort, whimper, belch, scream, squeak, roar and hiss, with effects that range from rude to amusing. When keeping

Elephant seals have the sensitive whiskers and teeth of a typical carnivore. They swallow most of their prey – such as dogfish shark (pictured left) – in one gulp.

Noses show who's boss in an elephant seal rookery. The size of a bull's nose and the magnificence of his vocal threats discourage rivals and help avoid actual battles. This in turn saves energy. These huge animals do not eat or drink for up to three months, so conserving energy is highly important. At Año Nuevo, it is easy to observe animals both in action and at rest.

track of their pups, females give a gentle maternal call. When arguing with their neighbors or being accosted by an unwelcome male, females produce a loud, retching gargle. Pups have their own vocabulary of sounds: they snap, mew, yip and whine for milk. When separated from their mothers, as is often the case in the confusion of the group, they have a distinctive treble siren which they add to the general din. Honors for most bizarre vocals must go to the adult male, however. Vocalizing from his throat, the male produces a series of booming snorts that carry for half a mile or more. This cry has been likened to a foghorn, a tom-tom, or a hammer hitting a hollow log. To me, it sounds like someone warming up a chainsaw, a rhythmic succession of almost-mechanical blips and burps. Even in person, it's hard to believe these sounds are issuing from an animal and not a Moog synthesizer.

Researchers have discovered that each rookery or breeding area of elephant seals has its own "dialect." New arrivals from another rookery soon learn to snort, whimper, belch, scream, etc., in that "dialect."

What are these animals communicating about? Many of the male-to-male noises are threats or challenges. Theirs is a society

Elephant
Seals

Visitors to Año Nuevo
State Reserve have a
ringside seat as two
well-matched bulls
battle for dominance.
At least 20 feet
between humans
and elephant seals
is required by law,
to avoid disturbing
the animals and
for visitors' safety.

Elephant Seals

To learn more about elephant seals, researchers at Año Nuevo track individual animals by tagging them and then marking them with harmless solutions. Each year when the animal molts, these "name tags" are shed and must be reapplied. Hundreds of animals have been named and studied in this fashion. As the photo indicates, elephant seals are very approachable most of the time, a factor which led to their near-extinction in 1892.

where males compete fiercely over females, and noises help intimidate the competition and avoid combat. Females have their own squabbles, and often quarrel with others over lost pups, invasion of space, unwelcome male attention, pups who are milk thieves, and so on. Pups vocalize to keep in touch with their mothers and to protest all the indignities they are constantly subjected to. Besides the growls and bites they get from someone else's mother, they are often tumbled or trampled by adult males en route to a battle or an amorous occasion.

Despite their bulk, elephant seals can move swiftly. When male rivals sound a challenge and undulate towards one another, they look like a pair of kingsize traveling waterbeds. Most of their mobility comes from an extremely flexible backbone, which allows them to lift their great

The mating game: battles between males for access to females occur within the harems at times. Thick skin on the animals' chest shields prevent major injury. Victorious males try to breed with as many females as they can. Females who are not ready for mating will reject male advances by kicking sand and giving a raucous protest cry.

bodies and hunch forward with the help of their foreflippers. Young or old, elephant seals can make their way quite a distance inland and climb sand dunes that are steep even by human standards.

Like other pinnipeds, elephant seals possess large eyes which see well on land and underwater. The pupil can expand quickly and hugely and the 3-inch eye contains a high concentration of rods, enabling it to make out shapes in low light. Pinnipeds don't have tear ducts. On land, this makes them appear to be crying. The "tears" are normal secretions to protect the eyes from salt and sand. Pinnipeds also have a membrane at the back of the eye to help see at night. Underwater, their eyes glow violet, just as cats' eyes do.

About two-thirds of the year, elephant seals live solitary sea-going lives, swimming and feeding miles from shore. December through March, elephant seals come together on land to breed and give birth. Most of their rookeries are remote, such as the Farallon Islands off San Francisco, and San Miguel Island in the Santa Barbara Channel. But at Año Nuevo in San Mateo County, California, we are privileged to witness their life cycle on the mainland.

It begins in late November with the arrival of breeding age males. They come ashore, fit and fat, surging with hormones and ready to do battle. They begin to challenge one another, issuing vocal threats and displaying their noses. Most fights end right there, once a less endowed bull sees his rival's proboscis.

hen bulls do fight, they rear up, chest to chest, biting, grappling and shoving. The battles look bloodier and more ferocious than they actually are. Chest shields of thickened skin and scar tissue protect the males from serious damage. Battles usually last just a few minutes, often ending with a decisive nose bite. Major battles between equally matched males can last half an hour, however. They often start on land and end with the loser being driven off into the ocean.

Winners of these battles eventually establish a pecking order, called a dominance hierarchy. The males with the longest string of victories are called alpha bulls. They tend to be the biggest animals with the largest noses, and are generally at prime breeding age – eight to 11 years.

By the time the females arrive in mid-December, the bulls have sorted themselves out into dominant or alpha bulls and marginal males. Because they are in the last stages of pregnancy, the females gather together in groups called harems. Each harem has an alpha bull who keeps other males away.

Three to six days after hauling out, each female gives birth to a single pup, 65 to 90 pounds. The mother's first action is to sniff her pup and warble at it. The pup warbles back. In the crowded confusion of the elephant seal rookery, this imprinting of newborn and mother is essential. Without it, a mother may fail to recognize her own pup and it will starve. Although born with its eyes open, the pup is wobbly and cannot swim or find its own food.

Pups nurse greedily and often. Their wrinkled, too-large black coats soon begin to fill out with fat. In four weeks, pups quadruple their birth weight. At the same time their mothers, who are fasting, visibly shrink. For each pound gained by the pup, the mother loses two.

Despite frequent nursing, a pup's life is not easy. Elephant seal mothers can do little to protect their offspring from unfriendly adults or accidents. If caught between two battling males, or in the path of a male who wants to mate with its mother, it is possible for a pup to get crushed.

Although nursing, females also come into estrus or heat for four days at the end of this period. As they come into estrus, they are mated

Mating between elephant seals is a swift affair, and preliminaries are few. The male slings his flipper (and his large nose or proboscis) over a receptive female and bites her neck. The female sometimes responds with a vocalization.

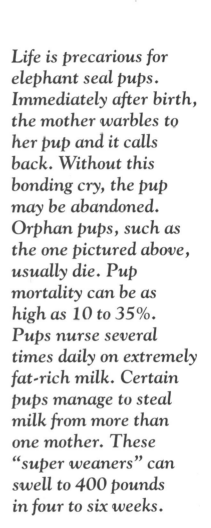

Life is precarious for elephant seal pups. Immediately after birth, the mother warbles to her pup and it calls back. Without this bonding cry, the pup may be abandoned. Orphan pups, such as the one pictured above, usually die. Pup mortality can be as high as 10 to 35%. Pups nurse several times daily on extremely fat-rich milk. Certain pups manage to steal milk from more than one mother. These "super weaners" can swell to 400 pounds in four to six weeks.

with by the alpha bull that controls their harem. Harem groups each contain from 25 to 50 females. Research has shown that these groupings are protected by the alpha bull but not really dominated by him. If a female group gradually moves to another part of the beach, the alpha male of that harem simply follows them and repositions himself.

Elephant seal bulls do not fight to defend a specific territory but to establish dominance with each other, and thus gain breeding access to the maximum number of females. Because the alpha male's primary goal is to mate with as many cows as possible, he does not eat during this entire 90-day period. He may mate as many as 200 times.

With this kind of sexual volume, courtship and other niceties are minimal. The male slings his flipper across the female, bites her neck and mates. If she protests, he bites her harder and puts his weight on her.

Despite his virility and wakefulness, the alpha bull is not able to guard the females on the outside edges of his harem as well as he would like. So he often lets a few subdominant males hang around the periphery, where they eye the females and attempt to mate with them when the alpha male is busy or resting. These "beta" bulls serve a useful function; by keeping lesser bulls away, they help save the alpha bull's energy.

When not in estrus, or when approached by a male they do not regard as alpha material, females launch a protest squawk that can be heard by the dominant bull even if he were in the next county. Other females in the group often take up the protest cry.

With this kind of activity, elephant seal rookeries exhibit periods of pandemonium. It is an amazing display of energy, especially given the fact that the only ones getting any food or drink are the pups. Elephant seals also have energy-saving strategies which they use to get them through this intense period. They rest frequently, and can stop breathing up to 30 minutes while sleeping.

Once pups are weaned, they group together in pods to learn to swim and to catch their own prey. Males soon begin to scuffle in mock battles to prepare them for the competition for dominance that will come at sexual maturity.

About a month after birth, pups are abruptly weaned. Their mothers simply head for the water. It may take them awhile to escape; still-ardent bulls try to stop them all the way into the sea. The alpha bull normally does little to protect the female at this point. This is one of the few mating opportunities available to the subdominant males, who often cruise vainly just offshore.

By March, most adults of both sexes, very much worse for wear, have departed for the sea. There they feed for several months and gain strength and poundage.

Meanwhile, the just-weaned pups remain on land. Clustered together in roly-poly groups called pods, the weaners slowly teach themselves to swim and catch prey. Their coats change from black to silvery-gray after weaning, which keeps them cooler. Between March and May, the weaners leave land for the open sea.

Around May, adult females return to shore for their molt. Large patches of skin and chunks of hair come out at a time, giving the animals a tattered appearance. Other animals molt, but the elephant seal goes through a "catastrophic molt." During this month, females sleep a great deal and fast once again.

As females leave with their new coats, the adult males arrive for their July-August molt. While they are molting, males lie close together in great groups, later moving into the water to swim, vocalize, and carry out friendly mock battles. By late August, almost all the elephant seals have left the land, and will not be seen again en masse until November.

*W*hile on land, elephant seals habitually toss sand over their broad backs. They are the only pinniped to engage in this behavior, using their small but agile foreflippers to make a fountain of sand which they lie under. They may do this to protect their skin, out of nervousness or habit, or to cool themselves.

As befits an animal of this size and activity, the elephant seal (when not fasting) eats heartily, diving deep into the ocean to catch its prey. The animals have been recorded in dives to 2,100 feet. Like other pinnipeds, they can hold their breath for up to 30 minutes, and can dive repeatedly without tiring.

Elephant seals eat bottom fish, rays, small sharks and invertebrates. Their biggest diet item is squid. It accounts for about 75% of the food they consume. To meet its high energy needs, and possibly to help cope with swallowing its prey whole, the elephant seal has intestines of an astonishing length. Some have measured over 600 feet – 25 times the length of the animal.

Elephant seal society is engrossing to watch, partly because there is so much to see and partly because the seals allow us to see it. In most instances, the animals are largely indifferent to us – quite a compliment, considering the way in which we methodically slaughtered them to near-extinction levels in the last century.

Nineteenth-century science operated on premises as odd as the elephant seals themselves. In 1892, when a group of scientists went to Guadalupe Island and found what they thought were the very last eight elephant seals in existence, they killed seven of them. What could have been their reasoning? A desire to have a few pickled specimens for the files, one supposes. Fortunately, they did not discover a group of elephant seals which must have been hiding. If they had, we would regret it very much. A world without the lovable oddity of the elephant seal would be a much poorer place.

Pinnipeds and other marine creatures suffer from manmade pollution, which ranges from oil contamination to entanglement in nets and plastic debris.

The annual molt for elephant seals takes place at different times for males, females and juveniles. Although the animals may appear ill, it is a natural process. Well-meaning humans sometimes try to "help" elephant seals in this state. Despite their docility, elephant seals are wild animals and should never be touched except by professionals such as these researchers, (pictured right) measuring a female.

ABOUT THE PHOTOGRAPHER

Naturalist-photographer **Frank Balthis** has worked extensively with pinnipeds and other seashore life for most of the last decade. From the remote islands off Baja California to the rookeries and hauling-out spots along the Golden State's shoreline, Frank has gained a sensitive understanding of pinniped behavior. He has worked as a park ranger at Point Reyes National Seashore, Año Nuevo State Reserve, and Yellowstone National Park. He has also served as naturalist for California Pacific Expeditions. His photos have appeared in publications of the National Geographic Society, the National Wildlife Federation, the Oceanic Society, Defenders of Wildlife, the Audubon Society and the Sierra Club. In addition, Frank is publisher-editor of *Mirounga, A Guide to Elephant Seals*, and several children's books. Thirty-one of his photos grace this book, including the cover shot of a young elephant seal.

ADDITIONAL PHOTOGRAPHERS

◆ **Ralph A. Clevenger**:
page 7, page 8
◆ **Howard Hall**:
title page, page 12, pages 18-19
◆ **Richard Hansen**:
page 2, page 4
◆ **W.E. Townsend, Jr.**:
pages 10-11, page 14, back cover

SPECIAL THANKS

Michael Putman; Sheri Howe; the Año Nuevo Interpretive Association; California State Park Rangers; and the faculty and researchers at U.C. Santa Cruz Institute of Marine Science.

FOR FURTHER INFORMATION

◆ **Año Nuevo Interpretive Association**, New Year's Creek Road, Pescadero, California 94060. Phone (415) 879-0454.

◆ **California Marine Mammal Center,** Marin Headlands-GGNRA, Fort Cronkhite, California 94965.

◆ **Friends of the Sea Lion,** 20612 Laguna Canyon Road, Laguna Beach, California 92651. Phone (714) 494-3050.

◆ **Recommended reading**: *Mirounga, A Guide to Elephant Seals*, by Sheri Howe; *Natural History of Año Nuevo*, by Leboeuf and Kaza; and *Marine Mammals*, edited by Delphine Haley.

ELEPHANT SEAL-WATCHING CALENDAR

The only mainland site where the public can see elephant seals in the wild is at Año Nuevo State Reserve, 75 miles south of San Francisco, California, on Highway One. Call (415) 879-0454 for hours and details of ranger-guided tours. The following is a general guide to activities throughout the year; naturally, there is some overlap.

◆ **November**: first bulls arrive on land; males battle for dominance; yearlings arrive

◆ **December**: females arrive; first pups born; lots of male battles

◆ **January**: more births; pups nursing; mating activities

◆ **February:** pups nursing; mating; first females leave and weaning begins

◆ **March**: all pups weaned; most adults gone by end of month; weaners learning to swim

◆ **April**: weaners on beach; juveniles and females arrive to molt

◆ **May:** continued molting by juveniles and females

◆ **June**: female/juvenile molt finished; males begin arriving

◆ **July**: males and sub-adults molt

◆ **August**: last of male molt; males begin to leave

◆ **September**: a few yearlings left on beach

◆ **October**: almost no animals on land

If you liked this book, we know you'll enjoy
others in our nature series, including:
A Pod of Gray Whales ❖ *A Pod of Killer Whales*
A Raft of Sea Otters ❖ *Sharks*
Hawks, Owls & Other Birds of Prey
A Dazzle of Hummingbirds ❖ *Parrots, Macaws & Cockatoos*

The Habitat series:
Tidepools ❖ *Coral Reefs* ❖ *Kelp Forest* ❖ *Icebergs & Glaciers*

SILVER BURDETT PRESS

© 1995 Silver Burdett Press
Published by Silver Burdett Press.
A Simon & Schuster Company
299 Jefferson Road,
Parsippany, NJ 07054
Printed in the United States of America
10 9 8 7 6 5 4 3 2 1